IMAGES
of America

CLIFTON PARK

Ferris wheel at Luna Park, Rexford, c. 1906. An amusement park existed at Rexford from 1906 to 1933.

COVER PHOTOGRAPH: Picnickers on the bridge over the sluice-way to the Vischer Mill, Vischer Ferry, July 4, 1891 (see p. 106).

IMAGES
of America

CLIFTON PARK

John L. Scherer

ARCADIA

First published 1996
Copyright © John L. Scherer, 1996

ISBN 0-7524-0409-1

Published by Arcadia Publishing,
an imprint of the Chalford Publishing Corporation
One Washington Center, Dover, New Hampshire 03820
Printed in Great Britain

Library of Congress Cataloging-in-Publication Data applied for

*Many of the photographs in this book
were collected by former Clifton Park Town Historian,
Howard I. Becker (1894–1978).
Without his foresight and interminable interest in town history,
much would have been lost. Howard collected these photographs,
including the Parker Goodfellow postcard collection, from 1935 to 1978.
He was also my friend and mentor.
I dedicate this book to him.*

Pair of oxen in front of the Clifton Park Hotel, Old Route 146 and Route 9, Clifton Park Village, c. 1890.

Contents

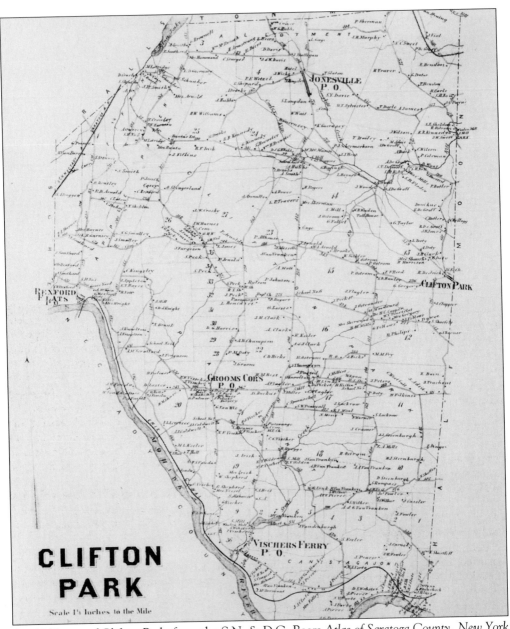

CLIFTON PARK

Scale 1½ Inches to the Mile

An 1866 map of Clifton Park, from the S.N. & D.G. Beers *Atlas of Saratoga County, New York* (1878), showing the Mohawk River along the south and west border of the town. The Erie Canal is the black line that parallels the river. The southern tip of Ballston Lake can be seen at the northwest corner of the map. The principal hamlets are also indicated. Those hamlets not indicated on the map, but referred to in the text, are: Clutes Dry Dock, on the Erie Canal in the southeast corner of the map; Forts Ferry, on the Mohawk River just west of Clutes Dry Dock; Elnora, known as Hubbs Corners in 1866, just south of Jonesville; and Clifton Park Center, the next intersection north of Grooms Corners. Many of the buildings depicted in the book can be found on this map.

Introduction

The art of photography brings the past alive. We come face to face with people like ourselves who lived in different times. We can see places and events that no longer exist, or that looked very different than they do today. There is no greater time machine. Photography developed in the mid-1800s and began to flourish by the end of that century. This collection of photographs, most of which were taken between 1875 to 1950, records the history of the town of Clifton Park, New York.

This book is about people; both present and former residents of Clifton Park. It is also about places and events in Clifton Park's history. The people who lived here were partially shaped by the area in which they lived. Although they lived in the "good old days," lacking the technology and modern conveniences of today's society, their lives were not so very different from our own. They went to school, worked hard, played, traveled from place to place, congregated at the local store, walked down tree-lined Main Streets, had family picnics, and celebrated Independence Day.

The town of Clifton Park was formed from the town of Halfmoon in 1828. It was the last town to be formed in Saratoga County. The town name was taken from the Clifton Park Patent, granted by Queen Anne of England in 1708. This patent had contained most of the land that comprised the area of the new town.

Transportation played an important role in the development of the area. The first settlement occurred in 1672 along the banks of the Mohawk River, one of the main sources of transportation and communication between settlements during the seventeenth and eighteenth centuries. This settlement was originally called Canastigione, an Indian word meaning "corn flats." It later became known as Fort's Ferry, after Nicholas Fort, who established a ferry across the river there in 1728.

A couple miles west of Fort's Ferry, also on the Mohawk, Eldert Vischer established a ferry in about 1790. The settlement that evolved here became known as Vischer's Ferry. While the river and ferries encouraged settlement of the southern areas of Clifton Park, roads and turnpikes were effecting settlement elsewhere. The Waterford-Saratoga Turnpike, which opened about 1820, saw taverns constructed along its route at what would later become Jonesville and Clifton Park Village. Today a section of this turnpike is still known as Plank Road, because boards were placed along the road to prevent it from becoming impassible during wet seasons. Another tavern was built by Samuel Grooms about 1820 at the corners that now bear his name. It was in this building that Clifton Park's first town board meeting was held in 1828.

The Erie Canal skirted the southern portion of the town. It was completed in 1825. The villages along its route expanded and thrived due to the business the canal created. A small settlement in the western part of the town, begun by Edward Rexford about the time of the American Revolution, contained an aqueduct (which carried the canal across the Mohawk River), two canal locks, a large hotel, and several canal stores. Vischer Ferry boasted two dry docks where canal boats were built and repaired. Clutes Dry Dock, a small hamlet on the eastern border of town, owed its existence to the canal. An influx of carpenters and other canal workers rapidly increased the town's population.

The railroad appeared in the northern part of town, and by the 1880s a freight depot was established at the railroad crossing. The business which the railroad brought encouraged a settlement named Hubbs Corners after an early settler in the area. However, the name of this settlement was changed to Elnora in 1882 when C.D. Hammond, supervisor of the D&H Railroad, named the community for his wife. By the early 1900s, another form of rail transportation had entered the town. The electric trolley brought people from Schenectady to an amusement park at Rexford.

The advent of the automobile would cause the next major spurt of growth in Clifton Park. This happened in 1965 when the Adirondack Northway opened, and made it possible for residents to commute to jobs in Albany. This soon became the era of tract housing and the cause of Clifton Park's continued growth and population boom.

For now, let's return to a pre-Northway Clifton Park, when agriculture was the primary occupation, roads were dirt, and the population was more like 3,000, rather than 35,000. Most of the photographs featured in this book are from the collections of the Town of Clifton Park. Many are postcard views taken between 1905 and 1915 by Schenectady photographer Parker Goodfellow. Goodfellow traveled throughout Clifton Park on his motorcycle, making postcard views and selling them to the various hotels and general stores located in town, where they were retailed to local residents and tourists.

The town's collection of photographs has been augmented by several private collections, generously made available to make this visual history more complete. Copies of these photographs have now been added to the town's collection.

The photographs are organized into six thematic chapters. Within these chapters the photographs are organized by location, usually starting in the south portion of town with the Forts Ferry area and proceeding in the following order: Clutes Dry Dock, Vischer Ferry, Grooms Corners, Rexford, Ballston Lake, Clifton Park Center, Elnora, Jonesville, and Clifton Park Village.

As you scan the pages of this book, I invite you to use a magnifying glass to explore details. It is amazing what can be discerned in this manner. Photographs are truly wonderful documents! Most of the requests made of the town historian are for early photographs of Clifton Park. I am delighted to at last make them available through this publication.

John L. Scherer
Vischer Ferry, New York
August 1996

One

Homesteads and Settlers

Nash House, across from the church, Clifton Park Center, c. 1890. The Nash family is posed in front of their farmhouse. From left to right: (front row, seated) Lydia Benedict Nash, Alva Nash (husband of Lydia Benedict), Abby Nash Peck, Guy Peck, John Foote Peck (husband of Abby Nash), and Harriet Peck; (back row, standing) Andrew Nash, Charles Nash, Miss Ide (a boarder), unknown, and Miss Selmer (a boarder). Families were proud of their homes, and from the early days of photography in the 1860s to the 1920s, families would often have their photographs taken in front of their houses. These photographs provide wonderful documentation of the early families and homesteads of Clifton Park.

Forts Ferry on the north shore of the Mohawk River, *c.* 1910. The ferry scow is in the foreground, and Mr. Lasher, the ferry man, is on the right. The Lasher House is in the distance. The ferry was a rope ferry, guided by a rope strung across the river. It was begun by Nicholas Fort in 1728. Just to the left was a well where it is said George Washington had a drink on his way from Ballston to Schenectady in 1783.

Pearse-Painter House, Forts Ferry, *c.* 1914. Mattie Clark is on the left and Grace Painter is next to her. They were daughters of Tunis and Mary Pearse. The woman seated may be Mary, or possibly Hattie Clute. First settled in the 1670s, by 1765 there were thirteen houses at this location, including the one pictured. This structure was burned by vandals in 1972; it was the last surviving home at Forts Ferry.

Fort House, Forts Ferry, *c*. 1914. Esther (seated, left) and Rachel Fort (standing, right) are on the porch. This home, built about 1850, was the last house owned by the Fort family along the river. After the river was dammed for the Barge Canal in 1907, frequent flooding forced the abandonment of Forts Ferry. Although the State of New York now owned the land, families were allowed permits to retain use of their houses, which became primarily summer homes. This house fell apart between 1940 and 1950.

Nicholas J. Clute, seated in a cutter in front of his home on the canal, Clutes Dry Dock, *c*. 1890. Clute owned and operated a dry dock and an adjacent store. Note the stonework of the canal.

Adam Van Vranken (1788–1880). Adam was a descendant of one of Clifton Park's first settlers. He and his brothers owned most of the land east of Vischer Ferry, which they inherited from their ancestors. Adam's first wife was Catherine Whitbeck, and his following two wives were Catherine's sisters. He was the last member of the Van Vranken family who could still speak Dutch.

Adam Van Vranken House, Erie Canal, east of Vischer Ferry, c. 1910. Adam and Catherine Whitbeck Van Vranken lived in this home on the banks of the Erie Canal. The house was certainly standing by 1825, and may have been built as early as the eighteenth century by Adam's father or grandfather. It was a favorite stop for hobos traveling on the towpath, as Mrs. Van Vranken never refused them a meal. Note the stonework of the canal in the foreground. The house was taken down in 1945, when architectural elements were used by George Buffoni to build a new house on Riverview Road.

John W. Van Vranken House, Riverview Road, east of Vischer Ferry, *c.* 1875. Dorcas Cragier Van Vranken is seated in the door; her son, William Halloway, and his wife, Susan Fort, are shown with their son Frank. John Whitbeck and Dorcas Craiger Van Vranken built this house in 1847. John was the town justice throughout the 1850s.

John W. Van Vranken House, Riverview Road, east of Vischer Ferry, *c.* 1900. William Halloway, Susan Fort Van Vranken, and their children are shown by the house. This is the same house as in the preceding photograph, but it was remodeled with a Victorian flair about 1885. In the early 1900s, it served as a boardinghouse for visiting tourists.

Vischer House, Ferry Drive, Vischer Ferry, *c*. 1910. The rear wing of this house (not seen) was built by Nicholas and Annette Vischer in about 1740. Their son Eldert built the imposing front section in about 1806. A penny with an 1806 date was found in one of the walls. Ferry Drive and the Vischer Mill can be seen on the left.

William Peters House, Crescent and Vischer Ferry Road, Vischer Ferry, *c*. 1910. This house was constructed in about 1814 by William and Jenett Peters. William was a miller, and his mill can be seen through the trees, to the right of the stone bridge (see p. 91). The stone bridge still exists.

Cornelius Hegeman House, Eric's Lane, Vischer Ferry, *c.* 1910. This house was built about 1829 by Cornelius and Margaret Hegeman. It was later owned by their son Christopher. By 1945, Christopher was operating a canal dry dock in front of the house. The building was moved to Route 9, Loudonville, in 1910 by Dr. L. Whittington Gorham.

Hegeman Tenant House with Mrs. Sherman on the porch, Riverview Road, Vischer Ferry, *c.* 1885. In the 1840s, Christopher Hegeman constructed three tenant houses along the south side of Riverview Road to house the boat builders and carpenters that worked at his dry dock. The home is still owned by descendants of the Hegeman family.

James Fort House, Riverview Road, Vischer Ferry, c. 1880. James Fort and his family are shown here outside their house. James was a carriage maker. The house stood on the north side of Riverview Road between the Stony Creek and the sluice way to the Vischer Mill.

Moses Van Vranken House, Crescent Road, near Vischer Ferry, c. 1875. Moses and Mary Van Vranken probably built this house about 1825. Jerome Van Vranken later lived here.

Andrew Vandenburg House, Crescent Road, *c.* 1880. Andrew (1838–1923) and Anna Chamberlain Vandenburg are shown by the pump next to their house. This brick Federal house stood on the south side of Crescent Road, just west of Bonneau Road. It burned down in 1942. The house features a fan light over the front door and an attached barn to the rear. According to early maps, this house was probably built by businessman Samuel Wilber and his wife Margaret in about 1820.

Abraham Best House, Vischer Ferry Road, near Vischer Ferry, August, 1890. This oil painting is signed by Ophelia L. Main, a granddaughter of Abraham (1790–1871) and Harriet Best, who built this house in 1815. The window shutters are all closed against the hot summer sun. The Best family came from Claverack, Columbia County, New York.

Nanning Irish House, Vischer Ferry Road, near Vischer Ferry, c. 1880. The family of Nanning and Kesiah Van Derwerken Irish are posed in front of their home. Pictured are: Nanning Irish (with beard); his mother, Sarah Clute Irish (seated); his wife, Kesiah Irish (at left); and their children, Sarah, Frances, and Albert. Note the steps used for getting in and out of the family carriage. The house was constructed about 1842.

Abner Irish House, Vischer Ferry Road, near Vischer Ferry, c. 1875. This is possibly John Irish (1837–1918) and his wife, Mary Cronkhite, with their daughter. The house, built about 1795 by Abner (1748–1825) and Thankful Irish of Amenia, Dutchess County, is just north of the Nanning Irish House. Their son Smiton inherited the house, as did Smiton's son, Benjamin F. Irish. By 1866, Smiton's grandson John owned the house. John was a son of Abner Irish (1807–1849) and Mary Clute. His brother, Nanning Irish, owned the neighboring farm, pictured at the top of this page.

Francis Vischer House, Stony Creek Reservoir, c. 1950. Francis Vischer built this home on the banks of the Stony Creek in 1813. It was undoubtedly built by the same men who built the Best House, two years later (see p. 17). This house was moved to Pheasant Lane, Loudonville, in 1950, due to the creation of the Stony Creek Reservoir.

Cornelius Van Vranken House, Stony Creek Reservoir, c. 1875. Built by James Weldon in about 1845, this house descended to a Weldon daughter who married Peter Van Vranken. Their son Cornelius is shown here with his house and family. The house was isolated on an island by the Stony Creek Reservoir, and it burned in 1968.

Nicholas Vischer House, Grooms Corners, c. 1920, now King Crest Farm. Hazel Gillette (on the steps at right), her parents, George and Belle, and other members of the Gillette family are sitting on the porch. The house was built about 1801 by Nicholas and Catherine Van Vranken Vischer, who were married that year.

Shopmyer House, Droms Road, Grooms Corners, c. 1908. Posed in front of their home are, from left to right: Albert Shopmyer, Frederick William Shopmyer, Marie Ruhe Shopmyer, Elizabeth Ruhe, William Shopmyer Jr. (half hidden), and Anna Ruhe. Albert's and William Jr.'s brother, long-time town resident Edgar Shopmyer, had not yet been born when this photograph was taken. Elizabeth and Anna were Marie's sisters-in-law.

Shopmyer Barns, Droms Road, Grooms Corners, c. 1908. Frederick William Shopmyer is standing with several horses near the barn.

Wetmore-Smith House, Riverview Road near Grooms Road, Rexford, c. 1945. According to a dated foundation stone in the cellar, the front part of this house was built in 1838. Note the Gothic windows in the solarium at rear, and the Gothic front door. The house was remodeled in the 1950s. Martha L. Wetmore Smith ran a dairy and apple farm here for fifty years after her husband's death in 1875.

Nott House, Nott Road, Rexford, c. 1900. This early farmhouse was built about 1780 by Eldad Holmes. It was purchased in 1845 by Howard Nott, a son of Eliphalet Nott and president of Union College. Howard used the house as a summer home.

Cyrus Rexford House, Route 146 and Riverview Road, Rexford, c. 1900. Posed in front of the house are three generations: Hannah Minerva Hollister Rexford (seated in the wheelchair); her daughter, Fanny Rexford Graves (standing in the center); and Fanny's daughters, Rita and Hollie (on either side of Fanny). This grand Victorian mansion was built by Cyrus and Hannah Rexford in 1883. Cyrus was a store owner, postmaster, and town supervisor. He incorporated an earlier farmhouse built by his ancestor, Edward Rexford, into the structure of this house.

Rogers family on their farm near Rexford, c. 1900. John Rogers was a photographer who undoubtedly took some of the Rexford photographs included in this volume. He is shown here with his wife Eva and their daughter Dorothy.

Hiram McKain House, Riverview Road, Rexford, c. 1920. This large farmhouse with its awnings down against the summer sun was located on the site of the present Edison Club, erected in 1925.

Lewis Garnsey House, Garnsey Road, Rexford, 1878. Lewis Garnsey married Augusta Groom in 1859 when he was forty-nine years old. It may have been at this time that they built the house illustrated in this print from Nathaniel Sylvester's *History of Saratoga County* (1878). Sylvester indicates that Mr. Garnsey's residence "is one of the most beautiful in the county, and is much admired by all who have had the good fortune to see it." Note the beautifully landscaped grounds.

Nathan Garnsey (DeLong) House, Route 146, Rexford, c. 1875. The two ladies seated on the porch may be Margery H. Smalley (1822–1884), wife of Nathan G. Smalley; and perhaps her youngest daughter, Emma Smalley (1863–1931), who later married LeGrand Rexford. This house was built in 1791 by Nathan and Nancy Garnsey of Litchfield, Connecticut. The white marble stone in the chimney bears the date of construction.

Caldwell House, Route 146, Rexford, 1878. The entire farm complex can be seen in this 1878 print from Sylvester's *History of Saratoga County* (1878). The house was originally built by Levi and Ann Garnsey about 1830, but was later purchased by Barney and Sarah Caldwell in 1868. This farm has been operated by the Caldwell family for over one hundred years.

Joseph Arnold House, Route 146 and Tanner Roads, 1878. This house was built by Joseph and Mary Arnold in about 1800. Its center chimney design belies Joseph's Rhode Island roots. The floor plan of the house is identical to the Nathan Garnsey (DeLong) House of 1791. A son, Peter Arnold, was born here in 1803, and he later inherited the farm as pictured in this print from Sylvester's *History of Saratoga County* (1878). In about 1986, the Arnold House was moved to Hop City Road in Charlton.

The Castle, Ballston Lake, *c.* 1900. William Bliss Baker, a famous landscape artist, built this house on the east side of Ballston Lake in 1885. He died a year later in an ice-skating accident in Central Park, New York City. He was only twenty-seven. Baker's studio was in the third story with a balcony overlooking the lake. The house was next owned by Dr. Samuel Smith, who made a road to it, now known as East Side Drive.

David Schauber House, Old Schauber Road, Ballston Lake, *c.* 1900. David and Maphlet Budlong Schauber built this house in the northwest corner of town in 1806. David's father had immigrated from Germany to Schenectady. The Schaubers raised twelve children in the house, which remained in the family for 180 years.

Asa Clark House, Vischer Ferry Road near Clifton Park Center, c. 1910. Asa and Eliza Weeks Clark built this house about 1845 in the popular Gothic Revival style. The vertical board and battens on the front and the Gothic window above the door are indications of this style. Asa was the son of Cyrus Clark, who owned the adjoining farm. Since Asa and Eliza's children both died young; their farm was later owned by Asa's nephew, John P. Clark, and his wife Emeline.

Cyrus Clark House, Vischer Ferry Road near Clifton Park Center, c. 1880. Posed in front of their house are John M. and Maria Peck Clark (seated), and their children, from left to right: John P. Clark, Caroline Clark, Montgomery Clark, and Eliza Jane Clark. The house was built by John M. Clark's parents, Cyrus and Nancy Morehouse Clark, about 1820. When John M. Clark died in 1907, his son, John P. Clark, and his family moved into the farmhouse from the Asa Clark house next door.

Barney House, Barney Road, Clifton Knolls, c. 1940. This farmhouse stood near the present Clifton Knolls Club House. It was last owned by Vincent "Jimmy" Secada, a native Spaniard, who sold his farm to Robert Van Patten in the late 1950s. Secada gave the Spanish names to the roads of Clifton Knolls, the development that was built on his farm. Van Patten provided Secada with an apartment upstairs in his new Barney Road clubhouse.

James Hicks House, Barney and Moe Roads, c. 1890. An unidentified woman is standing between two bushes by the fence. This elaborate Federal home sporting a Palladian window was probably built about 1820. According to 1851 and 1866 maps, and the 1850 census, it was owned by James and Jane Hicks. The Doty and Fields families were the last owners. The house was destroyed for Clifton Knolls in 1967.

Four generations, *c.* 1895. Harriet Shepard (1816–1897, at right) was the daughter of William Shepard. She and her husband, Francis N. Vischer, lived at Grooms Corners in a house still standing on Miller Road, just north of the intersection. Harriet's daughter, Huldah Vischer (1848–1918), is seated on the left. She was the wife of Erastus Forte. Her daughter, Minnie Forte (1868–1926), is standing. Minnie married Roland J. Wood of Jonesville; their daughter, Alma Wood (1893–1985), is the little girl in the photograph. She married Elmer Bloodgood, also of Jonesville.

Roland J. Wood House, Main Street, Jonesville, *c.* 1900. Roland J. and Minnie Forte Wood lived in this house at the time this photograph was taken. Their daughter, Alma Wood (the child in the top photograph on this page), was married here to Elmer Bloodgood. Alma was the sister of long-time Jonesville resident Vernon Wood. The sign on the tree reads "Wiard Plows," and the wagon is loaded with barrels. The barns are now gone.

Unidentified house in Clifton Park Village, *c.* 1880. This is a typical house photograph of the period, with owners and family posed in front. The carved Victorian posts and trim of the porch are unusual, as is the fenced railing along the roof of the rear section. Note the hanging flowers on the rear porch. Practically every house had a picket fence at this time.

Irving Button House, Route 9, Clifton Park Village, *c.* 1890. From left to right are: (in carriage) Fred Button, son of Irving and Caroline Peck Button; Irving Button; Caroline Peck Button; their daughter, Vennie Button; Caroline's mother; and Elizabeth Gafney, a schoolteacher.

Two
Street Scenes

Old Route 146 (Fire Road), Clifton Park Village, c. 1910. This postcard view, by Schenectady photographer Parker Goodfellow, was taken from Route 9 looking west along the south side of Old Route 146. It was obviously a major event when the photographer appeared—everyone stopped and posed. Note the harness shop on the left. Goodfellow recorded the tree-shaded main streets of Clifton Park in numerous postcard views. This section features some of them.

North landing, Forts Ferry, in winter, c. 1900. When the river was frozen during the winter months, traffic crossed on the ice. In the foreground you can see the path made by horses and wagons. The ferry scow has been pulled up on the bank at left until spring. Also on the left is the Lasher House, and on the right is the Forts Ferry House. When the Barge Canal was built, the latter house was moved up on the Van Vranken Road, where it later burned.

Clutes Dry Dock, looking east along the Erie Canal towpath, c. 1900. The first building on the left is the residence of J. Moncton, followed by the residence of Joseph Morehead, then the dry dock, and finally Clute's store. Nicholas Clute's home is out of sight beyond the store. All that remains of this settlement today are the bridge abutments, the dry dock, and foundation holes. Moncton's and Morehead's homes were moved up to a drier Riverview Road when the Barge Canal opened.

Clutes Dry Dock, 1878. This print from Nathaniel Sylverter's *History of Saratoga County* (1878) shows the home of Nicholas and Louisa Sherman Clute on the right, the Clute store in the center, and the dry dock on the left. The culvert that drained the dry dock out under the canal can be seen on the left. Two brothers, Abram and Jacob Volweider, owned the dry dock before Nicholas Clute acquired it in 1852.

Clutes Dry Dock, c. 1905. The home of Nicholas and Louisa Clute is shown at left with the canal bridge in the foreground. It is a good view of a farmers bridge, provided when farmland was cut by the canal. If you look closely you can see a woman in the yard on the other side of the fence. Compare this photograph with the print above.

Riverview Road, looking east from the store, Vischer Ferry, c. 1910. This postcard view was taken at the intersection of Vischer Ferry and Riverview Roads. The meat market sign reads from the other direction. Left of the meat market is a harness shop, later used for a funeral director's office (see p. 44), and eventually as Vischer Ferry's first firehouse in 1947. Note the narrow dirt road with sidewalks on both sides.

Vischer Ferry Road, looking north from the store, Vischer Ferry, c. 1910. Although the picket fences are gone and the road is now paved, the three houses pictured are still standing. They were all built about 1850 when canal boat builders filled the hamlet. The home on the right was built by harness maker Isaac Mull, whose shop can be seen in the photograph at the top of the page.

Riverview Road, looking west from the store, Vischer Ferry, *c.* 1910. The bridge across the Stony Creek is in the foreground, while the Greek Revival house built by Captain John and Hester Vischer lies in the distance on the corner of Ferry Drive. The home on the left is now gone, but according to the 1866 map it was owned by wagon maker James Fort. A woman is sitting on the side porch.

Riverview Road, looking east from the church, Vischer Ferry, *c.* 1910. The church parsonage, which burned about 1955, is shown on the left. The house on the right still stands.

Riverview Road, looking west toward the church, c. 1910. The church sheds can be seen on the left in the distance. Churchgoers would own or rent stalls to house their horses while at church. Nineteenth-century deeds for these stalls are still extant. However, the church sheds are now gone.

Looking north along Sugar Hill Road toward Grooms Road, Grooms Corners, c. 1910. On the left is the original tavern of Samuel Groom, later a general store. It was known in recent times as Klingbeils, and then as the Emporium (see pp. 50 and 75). This postcard view was taken by Parker Goodfellow of Schenectady who traveled via motorcycle. His vehicle is parked next to the tree.

Grooms and Sugar Hill Roads, looking south down Sugar Hill Road, Grooms Corners, *c*. 1910. These homes, which still stand, are across the road from the Grooms Tavern.

Sugar Hill Road, looking north, Grooms Corners, *c*. 1910. The Grange Hall is the second building on the left (see p. 107). The road is lined with trees, probably elms. They helped drainage and kept dust down.

Route 146 near the bridge, Rexford, 1899. From left to right are: the early McLane Hotel, the blacksmith shop, and the Cyrus Rexford store. A peddler's wagon appears to be parked in front of the store. Between the hotel and blacksmith shop, a canal bridge can be seen. The Erie Canal ran in back of these buildings.

Route 146 near the bridge, Rexford, c. 1910. The Cyrus Rexford store is on the left, sporting a new porch. The canal and aqueduct can be seen to the rear of the buildings in the distance. The toll bridge runs to the right of the aqueduct. Note the tollhouse on the right.

Main Street, Rexford, c. 1910. This photograph was taken from in front of the Rexford Methodist Church. From left to right are: the Cornell home, the H. Cornell blacksmith shop (see p. 97), and Templars Hall.

Railroad crossing, Belott Road, Elnora, c. 1910. A train can be seen crossing the road in the distance. Molding sand appears to be piled on the left, ready to load onto the train. The mining of molding sand was a major town industry. The overpass replaced the crossing in the 1920s. This road is now a dead end.

Main Street (west side) at MacElroy Road, Jonesville, *c.* 1910. The Greek Revival house on the right was probably built about 1850. The third house from the right recently burned.

Main Street (west side), looking north from the church, Jonesville, *c.* 1910. These homes were built in the 1840s and 1850s. The first home on the left still stands, but the next two have been removed. Dyer Drive now runs through the site of the third house from the left.

Main Street (east side), looking south, Jonesville, *c*. 1910. A farm wagon approaches. The firehouse is now on the site of the first three houses on the left. The slanting fence on the right can be seen in the photograph below. The trees along the side of the road are probably elms.

Main Street (west side), looking south, Jonesville, *c*. 1910. This postcard view was taken from the same spot as the previous one, this time showing the opposite side of the road. The house on the right has been torn down, but the others still stand.

Old Route 146 (north side), looking east from Route 9, Clifton Park Village, *c.* 1910. The Clifton Park Hotel is out of sight, just to the left of this postcard view. This part of the village is in the town of Halfmoon. The town line basically follows Route 9.

Old Route 146 (north side), looking west toward Route 9, Clifton Park Village, *c.* 1910. In the distance on the right are the horse sheds for the Clifton Park Hotel. The hotel is just to the right of the sheds. Only a part of a column can be seen between the sheds and the tree. The sheds and part of the hotel are in the town of Clifton Park, while the foreground is in Halfmoon.

Three
Public Places

Store, corner of Main Street and Longkill Road, Jonesville, *c.* 1890. This is the Jonesville store as it looked before it was enlarged in about 1900 (see p. 63). It was probably built between 1845 and 1855. In the days before telephones and radios, people would gather at the general store to catch up on news and gossip. Note the plow in front of the store on the right, and the pump to water horses on the left.

Store and dry dock, on the Erie Canal at Clutes Dry Dock, c. 1900. The canal walls are in the foreground. At left are the wooden gates to the dry dock, where canal boats were built and repaired. Nicholas Clute's store is on the right. This all disappeared by the time the Barge Canal opened in 1917.

Funeral Directors, Riverview and Vischer Ferry Roads, Vischer Ferry, c. 1897. Garret Van Vranken (the owner) is standing in the door. He later took his brother Brower into the business (see p. 93). Since people were waked at home, a large funeral home was not needed. This building was originally a harness shop owned by Isaac Mull. In 1947, it became Vischer Ferry's first fire station. It was moved across the road and used as a home by Ried and Genevieve Briggs for many years.

Store and Post Office, Vischer Ferry, *c.* 1905. A store was first built at Vischer Ferry by Benjamin Mix. It was in operation on the site shown here by 1791, a date that appears on a grocery bill belonging to Derck Bradt. Mix's original store was probably incorporated into the present store.

Store, Vischer Ferry, *c.* 1955. Even before modern malls existed, kids would "hang out" at stores. The general store was operated by the Olsen family until about 1969. It has since been restored and is now a tack shop. Ordie Shippee and his father operated the store from 1914 to 1947. Ordie recalled that there were hardly any packaged goods, and that he often accepted goods in trade rather than money.

Hotel, Vischer Ferry, c. 1905. This hotel, built in 1797 by Benjamin Mix, replaced an earlier tavern built in 1787. It was a landmark in the hamlet until it burned in 1947. As a result of the fire, the Vischer Ferry Volunteer Fire Department was formed the same year. The fire station was eventually built on the site of the hotel. Brower Van Vranken's Funeral Office is visible through the trees on the left (see p. 44), as is the meat market (see p. 34).

"Good News Folks!"

Yes, Good News for Lovers of Fine Foods and Beverages

A Famous Old Establishment Welcomes You Again!

VISCHER'S FERRY HOTEL

— JERRY JAROME, Proprietor

"JERRY"

Jerry Jarome, well known business men and restaurateur, takes pride in presenting this famous hostelry to his many friends. His experience and reputation for fine foods and drinks insures complete satisfaction for present day patrons of Vischer's Ferry Hotel.

A Fine Old Bar

Here's a tap room that radiates real old fashioned hospitality. Here's the spot for friendly drinks of your favorite brand of fine liquors. When a drink is in order —make it at Vischer's Ferry Hotel.

VISCHER'S FERRY HOTEL
Famous Hostelry Since 1810

FULL COURSE STEAK or BROILER DINNERS 2.00

Served: Weekdays 5 to 9; Sundays 1 to 9

DINNER AT VISCHER'S FERRY HOTEL IS LIKE OPENING THE DOOR ON THOSE GOOD OLD DAYS. EXCELLENT FOOD, DELICIOUSLY COOKED AND SERVED IN THESE QUAINT OLD DINING ROOMS.

Your Favorite Drinks Superbly Mixed! Phone "JERRY" Schenectady 2-0781 A Banquet Here is a "BANQUET"

To Insure Your Complete Satisfaction - - - We Suggest "Reservations"

ALL ROADS LEAD TO VISCHER'S FERRY HOTEL

Broadside for the Vischer Ferry Hotel, 1946. This broadside was used for the hotel's last year of operation. The structure burned the following year. The photograph on the broadside shows that the hotel was spruced up with brickcote, a new wrap-around porch, and a lighted sign.

District School No. 3, Riverview Road, Vischer Ferry, c. 1890. The students are all dressed up for the photograph. Like most one-room schoolhouses, there was no running water or indoor pluming. The water was fetched from a neighboring house, and the toilets were "out back." There were separate entrances on either side of the porch for boys and girls. The bell would announce the beginning of the school day. The school was built about 1848, used until 1953, and is now a residence.

District School No. 3, Riverview Road, Vischer Ferry, c. 1905. A large pot-bellied stove is at left. George Washington can be seen peering from the back of the room, and the ever-present wall map is on the right. Students in kindergarten through eighth grade were taught here. The total number of students ranged from twenty-five to thirty, with class size ranging from as few as two or three students per grade to as many as six or eight at times.

Amity Reformed Church, Riverview Road, Vischer Ferry, c. 1860. This drawing depicts the original church, built in 1802. It faced east toward the present parking lot. The fenced cemetery can be seen on the hill behind. Notice the fish-shaped weather vane. The congregation gave the name Amity to the new community, but it never won out over Vischer Ferry.

Amity Reformed Church, Riverview Road, Vischer Ferry, c. 1880. This building replaced the earlier church in 1871. It now faced the road. You can see the horse sheds on the right. Other sheds were across the road (see p. 36). The pot-bellied stove overheated during the Christmas service of 1886, and the church burned.

48

Amity Reformed Church, Riverview Road, Vischer Ferry, *c.* 1905. The new church was completed in 1888. The architectural trim was accented by painting it a contrasting color. The stained-glass windows are striking features. The social hall on the left remained from the earlier building. Today, the church retains nearly all of its original appointments.

Canal store, Lock 19, Erie Canal, Vischer Ferry, *c.* 1900. This store on the north side of Erie Canal Lock 19 also served as the lock tender's house. The boy seated in the doorway is probably John Woodin. John was the last lock tender at Lock 19. He began this career by helping his father in 1896 at the age of six. At age twelve, John could operate the lock by himself.

Grooms Tavern, Grooms Corners, *c.* 1910. Built by Samuel Groom in about 1820, this tavern was the site of Clifton Park's first town board meeting in 1828. During the early years, the town board would meet at various taverns in town. In the twentieth century (*c.* 1918 to the early 1960s) the Klingbiel family operated a store in this building. There was a billiard parlor in the rear (see pp. 36 and 75).

Grooms Methodist Church, Vischer Ferry Road, *c.* 1955. Established in 1789, this was the third church building erected on the site. It was built in 1834. The interior was typical of simple meetinghouses, and boasted a generous "horseshoe" gallery. It was referred to as "The White Church." In about 1960, the congregation moved to a new building on Route 146, and the old church became a furniture store called "The Deacon's Bench." It burned in 1975.

District School No. 2, Sugar Hill and Ray Roads, Grooms Corners, *c.* 1924. From left to right are: (first row) Alta Harris, Clarissa Pierce, ? Pierce, ? Krosky, Doris Ray, Catherine Harris, Esther Ross, Jennie Oldorff, Dorothy Oldorff, Francis Groat, and Sophie Angle; (second row) Bill Groat, Edgar Shopmyer, Walter Moran, Paul Moran, Gert Angle, ? Sisson, unknown, Fred Droms, Herm Predel, Louretta Oldorff, and Mary Predel; (third row) unknown, Ed Moran, Ethel Blair, Dorothy Groat, Caroline Klingbeil, Elnora Brawn, Wreatha Harris, Allen Klingbeil, Charlie Van Arnam, and Charlie Oldorff; (back row) Marion Ray, Mary Oldorff, Florence Angle, teacher Elizabeth Brookley, Johanna Lippert, Florence Blair, Josephine Guilmette, and Edgar Van Olinda.

George Eaton Store, Main Street, Rexford, 1901. The boy on the box could not stay still for the photograph. This store was on the river side of Main Street, and it became Rexford's first firehouse in about 1928. When the old Rexford store was demolished in 1964 for the new road, Walt Esselborn moved his business, the Mohawk Market, to this location.

Cyrus Rexford Store, Erie Canal and Route 146, Rexford, c. 1890. From left to right, as identified on the photograph, are: Willie Connors, unknown, Jimmie the tinker, unknown, three Conley girls, Mattie Conley, Silas Burke, L.G. Rexford, unknown, Frank Connors (boy), and unknown. This photograph depicts the canal side of the store. A variety of goods can be seen inside and along the porch. Cyrus Rexford (1819–1900, see p. 22) may have owned the store as early as 1842. His son, LeGrand, took over the business. The store was demolished in 1964 for the new bridge and road.

Cyrus Rexford Store, Erie Canal and Route 146, Rexford, c. 1890. This photograph depicts the Route 146 side of the store (see p. 38). The store was also the post office and the store owner, Cyrus Rexford, was postmaster. People would often congregate at the local store, the shopping mall of its day.

Michael Travis Store, Lock 22, Erie Canal, Rexford, c. 1905. Michael Travis is undoubtedly in the photograph; perhaps he is the man on the right, or the one standing under the porch holding his vest. The top of Lock 22 can be seen in the foreground. This store was built about 1900. It is now the Schenectady Yacht Club.

McLane Hotel, Route 146, near the bridge, Rexford, c. 1953. This building replaced an earlier building c. 1900 (see p. 38). It was a popular watering hole for canallers.

Demolition of the McLane Hotel, Route 146, near the bridge, Rexford, 1964. The hotel was removed in 1964 to make way for a new bridge and road. Prior to this time the Rexford bridge actually crossed on the old aqueduct. Route 146 now crosses over the hotel site.

Rexford Methodist Church, Main Street, Rexford, c. 1900. The church was built in 1839. You can see the horse sheds on the right, used to shelter horses and buggies while people attended services. The sheds were also used by people who took the trolley to Schenectady.

Rexford Post Office, Route 146, near the bridge, Rexford, c. 1905. This is probably postmaster LeGrand Rexford (in the door) and his wife, Emma Smalley (center). The post office was in the Rexford store (see pp. 38, 52, and 53). Note the poster for Buffalo Bill's Wild West Show, featuring Annie Oakley.

District School No. 1, northeast corner of Route 146 and Riverview Roads, Rexford, 1893. Among those shown here are: teacher Anna McBride Schermerhorn (back row, far right), Eliphalet Nott (back row, second from right, the great grandson of the Union College president), Allan and James McKain, John Rogers, Frank Eaton, John and Mary Bennedict, Reeves and Octavia Congdon, and Andrew Scanlon. The school was condemned in 1905, moved across Route 146 to the north side of Riverview Road, and converted to a home.

District School No.1, northeast corner of Route 146 and Riverview Roads, Rexford, 1952. From left to right are: David Bennett, John Potter, Clark Wilson Jr., and Valerie Wilson. This two-room school, which replaced the earlier school in 1905, was replaced by the fire station in 1963.

District School No. 7, Route 146 at Waite Road, c. 1920. These girls are playing baseball outside the school. The girl on the left with the hat is Jeannette DeLong. The photograph was probably taken by her brother, LeGrand DeLong. Students would generally play games during recess until the teacher called them back to class with a hand bell. The school is now a residence.

District School No. 6, northeast corner of Vischer Ferry and Clifton Park Center Roads, 1942. From left to right are: Tom Klingbeil, ? Crowley, Alice Millington, unknown, Keith Peck, ? Crowley, Don Berthiamue, and three other unidentified students. The students made the quilt to send to a soldier in World War II. The school was near the site of the present town hall.

Clifton Park Baptist Church, Clifton Park Center, *c.* 1900. Founded by Abijah Peck in 1794, the church pictured was built in 1837, and features a large tub under the sanctuary where full immersion baptisms could take place. Abijah Peck (1757–1848), a weaver from Galway, is buried in back of the church.

Store, just west of the church, Clifton Park Center, *c.* 1910. The owners, members of the Losee family, are pictured in front of the store. Notice the scale in the doorway to weigh produce. A large scale to weigh hay wagons was located across the road. The store was last operated by Alice Losee in the late 1930s. It was converted to a house, and has been the home of Dr. Elizabeth Peck since 1944.

District No. 5 School, southwest corner of Moe and Grooms Roads, 1910. From left to right are: (front row) unknown, Matt Liedkie, unknown, unknown, Ed Carlson, unknown, Emil Carlson, unknown, Jake Hayes, and unknown; (middle row) George Carlson, Adam Herold, unknown, unknown, Carrie Hayes, Hattie Powell, Ida Englemore, Viola Hayes, Lizzie Liedkie, John Powell, unknown, unknown, and Miss Potts (teacher); (back row), Kate Myers, Anna Englemore, Edith Adsit (later a teacher, see below), and Mabel Carlson. This school, now a nursery school, was built in 1905.

District No. 5 School, southwest corner of Moe and Grooms Roads, 1952. From left to right are: (front row) unknown, unknown, unknown, Floyd ?, Beverly Blanchard, Robert Blanchard, Judith Carlson, unknown, Eleanor Morse, unknown, Catherine Connors, unknown, Kathleen Connors, unknown, unknown, Mary Ethel Bahr, Martha Donahue, Ken Flagler, Stephen Jarosz, Jimmy Jarosz, and unknown; (back row) unknown, Bob Herold, Gail Sauerbrey, Winnie Angier, Bruce Jerome, and unknown. The teacher is Mrs. Edith Adsit Allen, a student in the previous photograph. The school closed in 1953.

Smith's Grain and Feed Store, Elnora, *c.* 1910. This business was established in 1892 by Dibble and Hurlburt. It was purchased by George T. Smith in 1895, and until 1994, it was operated by four generations of the Smith family. Originally, Smith's store served the farm community by grinding corn and custom-blending molasses in it to make cattle feed. In later years it served as a hardware store.

Store and post office, Elnora, *c.* 1910. This store was known as Jump and Petersons throughout the 1930s, '40s, and '50s. Richard Jump started the business, and later took in Nelsen Peterson, who married Jump's daughter Lena. Richard Jump, and later Lena Peterson, served as postmasters. After the grocery business ceased, the postal functions were moved to the front of the store. Until the new Clifton Park Post Office was established in January 1976, many people in Clifton Park had an Elnora address.

Elnora Hotel, Belott Road, Elnora, *c.* 1910. The sign over the door reads: "G. G. Belott Elnora Hotel." The railroad tracks were just to the left. Because of the train station and freight depot, Elnora became a chief stopping-off place (see p. 39).

District School No. 10, Route 146A, Elnora, *c.* 1910. The two entrances for boys and girls are clearly visible. Grades one through eight were offered. The teacher would bring each class to a bench in front of the room to recite their lessons. There was no high school in Clifton Park until 1953. Prior to that time those who continued their education went to Cohoes, Mechanicville, or Niskayuna.

Hotel, Main Street and MacElroy Road, Jonesville, c. 1910. James Jones constructed this hotel along the Waterford-Saratoga Turnpike about 1820, and it was as a stop on the turnpike that the village developed. In 1848 the section of turnpike between Clifton Park Village and Jonesville was paved with wood planks to make it passable even in wet times. A toll was charged to use this Plank Road Turnpike. The hotel burned in 1915. The name on the sign is "Fitzgerald's," probably one of the last owners.

Odd Fellows Hall, Main Street, Jonesville, c. 1965. Fraternal organizations were ever-popular during the early twentieth century. This building provided the local chapter of Odd Fellows a place to meet and socialize. Annual poultry shows were held here during the 1920s and '30s. No doubt many other community events also took place here before the building was removed in the 1970s.

Store and post office, Main Street, Jonesville, *c.* 1900. This photograph was taken shortly after the store was remodeled and the roof raised (see p. 43). As with the other hamlets, the store also served as the post office. Note the storage shed to the left and the larger display windows.

Store and post office, Main Street, Jonesville, *c.* 1910. At the time this postcard view was taken by Parker Goodfellow, the store was owned by W.C. Shepard. Some oil lamps can be seen in the store window on the left. Note the pump at left, also visible in the photograph on p. 43. Down the road to the right a blacksmith shop and the entrance to the cemetery can be seen. To the right behind the blacksmith shop is a cemetery vault.

Jonesville Academy, Main Street, Jonesville, c. 1910. Built in 1836 as a private boarding school, the academy made provision for fifty boarders, male and female, and offered an academic, commercial, classical, and "ornamental" education. It was like a junior-senior high school. Board and tuition was $100 for an academic year of forty-four weeks. The academy closed in 1876, and until 1953 the building was used by the public school system as District No. 9. The school was sold in 1977 and it is now a residence. The bell is now at the Methodist church.

Academy dormitory and Episcopal church, Main Street, Jonesville, c. 1910. The building on the left was the girls dormitory for the Jonesville Academy. It was originally the Methodist church, c. 1826, which, when the present church was built in 1854 (see p. 122), was moved across the street to its present location for use as a dorm. This building was later a residence, and it is now apartments. The Episcopal church on the right was probably built during the 1870s, and is vacant today.

Fire station, Main Street, Jonesville, 1957. Jonesville's first fire station (in the foreground) was purchased in 1925 for $1,500. The building first served as a wagon shop. In 1956, the land behind was purchased for the building of a new station (shown in the rear).

Methodist church, north side of Old Route 146 (Fire Road) west of Route 9, Clifton Park Village, c. 1910. The church was built in 1842. The old Plank Road Turnpike to Jonesville can be seen to the left of the church. The road is now cut off by the Northway.

Store, southwest corner of Old Route 146 (Fire Road) and Route 9, Clifton Park Village, c. 1885. The locals are all gathered around the store of Jacob Boyce. Note the man seated at left reading a newspaper. The high-wheel bicycle on the right helps date the photograph. Note the butter churns and farm tools on the porch. The store was demolished when Route 9 was widened.

Store and post office, southwest corner of Old Route 146 (Fire Road) and Route 9, Clifton Park Village, c. 1910. The store of Jacob Boyce in the previous photograph is now being run by H. F. Barrett. The photographer's motorcycle is parked against the porch (see p. 36). The little shop on the right is an ice cream parlor, and the building only partially visible beyond that is a harness shop (see p. 31).

District School No. 12, south side Old Route 146 (Fire Road) west of Route 9, Clifton Park Village, c. 1910. This one-room school has been replaced by the Clifton Park Firehouse. The bell from its cupola, hidden behind the trees, is now in front of the firehouse. All the one-room schools in town were abandoned by 1953, when the new centralized campus was first used.

Hotel, northeast corner of Old Route 146 and Route 9, Clifton Park Village, *c.* 1880. This early tintype of the hotel shows what appears to be a peddler and his wagon. The back of the wagon is open to display his wares. Is the man with the white apron the peddler or the proprietor of the hotel? Another fancy wagon is in front of the horse sheds to the left. The Waterford-Saratoga Turnpike (now Route 9) came to the front of the hotel, then veered right toward Mechanicville or left toward Jonesville and Ballston Spa.

Hotel, northeast corner of Old Route 146 and Route 9, Clifton Park Village, *c.* 1910. Ephraim Stevens built the hotel in the 1820s. This stop on the Waterford-Saratoga Turnpike was known as Stevens Corners until the 1850s, when it became known as Clifton Park Village. Ephraim Stevens was the first supervisor of Clifton Park in 1828. The hotel was a focal point for community activities, including dancing and roller skating. It served as courthouse and jail, and town board meetings were often held here. The Clifton Park-Halfmoon town line passes through the center of the hotel.

Four
Transportation

Locomotive at Elnora Crossing, c. 1890. A railroad line crosses the town from Ushers, west to Elnora, and then travels south to near the Alplaus Creek to Glenville and Schenectady. This line was the result of an 1877 agreement between the Delaware and Hudson Railroad and the Boston, Hoosack Tunnel, and Western Railway Company. Elnora served as a freight depot for the D&H for many years. Another railroad, the Saratoga and Schenectady, crossed the western edge of town going north and south, passing through Ballston Lake. This railroad began service in 1832, and was our nation's second railroad.

Ferry scow at Forts Ferry, c. 1905. This typical rope ferry was guided across the Mohawk River by a cable. The cable is visible in this postcard view by Parker Goodfellow, as are the two drop cables that connect it to the scow. When one drop cable is longer than the other, the flow of water forces the ferry across. A long pole was used to push off from shore. The toll depended upon the number of axles on the vehicle, or the number of horses. This ferry was established by Nicholas Fort in 1728, and it operated until the Barge Canal opened.

Ferry scow at north landing, Vischer Ferry, c. 1910. People wait to cross the river, perhaps to catch the train at the Rosendale Station on the south side. Note the cable across the river and the two long poles which keep the steel cable from swinging across the scow scaring the horses or passengers. This ferry was established by Eldert Vischer in about 1790, and continued in operation until about 1923.

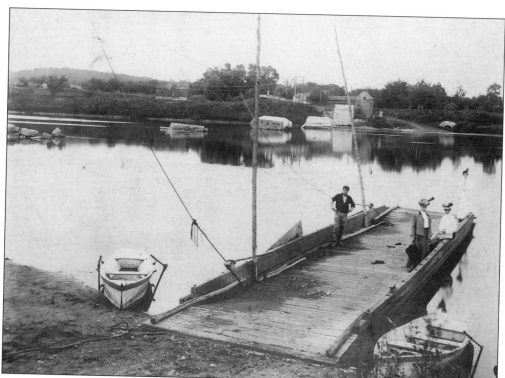

Ferry scow at south landing, Vischer Ferry, c. 1910. The man on the scow may be John Woodin (see p. 49) who operated the ferry from 1908 to 1915. The abutments and tollhouse for the 1900 bridge are visible (right), as is the culvert opening that carries the Stony Creek under the canal. The coal pocket (see p. 90), canal bridge (see p. 72), mill (see p. 91), and storehouse near the dry dock can also be seen.

Toll bridge, looking north, Vischer Ferry, 1901. Ed Wendt and A. Loucks are in the boat. This stereoview was taken by the Albany photographers, the Wendt Brothers. The bridge, financed locally, was built in 1900. In the spring of 1901, two sections of the bridge went out with the ice floods. It was raised some 3 feet, but in 1902, the spring floods carried the entire bridge away. Remains of the bridge are still dredged from the river.

Erie Canal at Vischer Ferry, *c*. 1890. The canal bridge was at the end of Ferry Drive. Two boats in tow are being pulled by three mules. The Erie Canal was dug through Clifton Park in 1822 by local labor, and when it opened in 1825, it provided a water route from the Hudson River to the Great Lakes. Early settlers passed through town on their way west.

Lock 19, Erie Canal, Vischer Ferry, c. 1900. John Woodin's father, who tended Lock 19 for many years, is on the left. We are looking east—the gates are open, and ready for a boat to enter. Once a boat entered the lock, the gates were closed and water was pumped out of the lock until the lower level was reached, then the lower gates were opened. In 1853, 175 boats per day passed through this lock. By 1875, the number had dwindled to 95 boats per day.

Lock 19, Erie Canal, looking west, Vischer Ferry, October 1907. This steam yacht was too large for the lock. A portion of the bow had to be removed, and the stack collapsed to fit under bridges. The canal was enlarged through Clifton Park in 1842, at which time this double chamber lock was constructed. In 1885 the northern chamber was lengthened to accommodate several boats in tow.

Excursion boat *Kittie West*, c. 1910. From left to right are: Mr. Foote, Mr. Quackenbush, and Frank Sargent. The *Kittie West* was an excursion boat from Schenectady that brought passengers to Rexford, Vischer Ferry, and Clutes Dry Dock along the old Erie Canal.

Excursion boat *Kittie West*, Erie Canal at Clutes Dry Dock, c. 1900. This photograph, taken in front of the store at Clutes Dry Dock, must depict some type of men's outing. There are no women on board. The *Kittie West* brought many a picnicker from Schenectady. A music box, now at the Schenectady Historical Society, provided entertainment on board.

Store, Grooms Corners, *c.* 1910. The automobile first appeared on Clifton Park roads at this time. Dr. Strang of Vischer Ferry was one of the first to own one of these new machines. He may be the man pictured in this Parker Goodfellow postcard view. The owner of the store (probably Jim Groom) is sitting on the porch. The building was formerly the Grooms tavern (see pp. 36 and 50). Ed Klingbiel purchased the store in about 1918 and ran it until the early 1960s.

Hazel Gillette, Grooms Corners, *c.* 1919. Hazel Gillette is sitting on a motorcycle belonging to her future husband, Chester Adams. The photograph was taken in back of her parents' home on Grooms Road, now King Crest Farm (see p. 20).

Erie Canal, feeder canal, Lock 21, and aqueduct, Rexford, *c.* 1880. This view from the cliff looking west was popular with photographers. The small canal on the left brings water into the main canal from the Mohawk River. Lock 21 is now a part of the Schenectady Yacht Club, and is used to lower boats into the water in the spring, and raise them out in the fall. In the distance is Rexford. Among the buildings that can be seen are: the Rexford Store; the old McLane Hotel; and to the right, the Methodist church without the bell tower. Many other interesting details can be explored in this rare, early photograph.

Erie Canal Aqueduct at Rexford, c. 1900. This is the east side of the aqueduct, which was actually a bridge that carried the canal across the Mohawk River. Another aqueduct at Crescent brought the Erie Canal into Saratoga County, where it continued for 13 miles before returning to the south side of the river at Rexford. The Rexford Store (see p. 52) is on the canal at the right, and the new McLane Hotel (see p. 54) is just in back of the store. Note the windmill next to the hotel.

Erie Canal Aqueduct at Rexford, c. 1900. The west side of the aqueduct shows the large, supporting arches that carried the canal over the river. The toll bridge for foot, horse, and carriage traffic is next to the aqueduct. The toll gate for the bridge can be seen at the north end, and just beyond is the McLane Hotel. Lock 22 is at the north end of the aqueduct, with the Rexford Store on the left and the Travis Store (see p. 53, now the Yacht Club) on the right.

Lock 22, Erie Canal, Rexford, *c.* 1905. This view was taken from the north end of the aqueduct looking east. The Travis Store is at the right. This double chamber lock could accommodate two canal boats at once going in either direction. Note the canal boat in the right chamber, and the wooden gates to the lock.

Waiting canal boats at Lock 21, Erie Canal, Rexford, *c.* 1912. These canal boats headed west must wait their turn to enter the lock. Canallers often fought one another to see who would enter the lock first. Some canallers even engaged expert fighters to travel with them to gain the upper edge. Many professional prize fighters got their start on the Erie Canal.

Tugboat *William Coleman* in Lock 22, Erie Canal, Rexford, *c.* 1910. The tugboat is headed east, and is thus being lowered in the lock. It appears to be pulling a barge. The Rexford Store is to the right.

Men, boy, and dog at Lock 22, Erie Canal, Rexford, *c.* 1910. This group is posed against the lever that operates the lock gate. The man on the left is Ullman "Ollie" R. Bartow, and the one on the right is Levi Benedict. The lock was a favorite place to congregate.

Girls watching a canal boat enter Lock 22, Erie Canal, Rexford, c. 1905. The boat is entering the lock from the east. The gates will close behind it, and the lock will be filled with water to raise the boat to the next level. The McKain farm, now the site of the Edison Club, can be seen at the top of the hill on the right. One of the girls on the left is carrying books—perhaps the they are on their way to or from school. The photograph was taken by John Rogers (see p. 23).

Electric trolley on bridge, Rexford, c. 1908. The electric trolley came from Schenectady to Luna Park, an amusement park in Rexford. It continued north to Ballston Lake, Ballston, and Saratoga. It crossed the Mohawk River on the longest trolley bridge in the world. The steel bridge was built in 1904 and dismantled about 1943, after trolley service was discontinued. The cement piers are still standing in the river.

RUINS BRIDGE AT AQUEDUCT (22)

Ruins of the toll bridge at Rexford, c. 1914. Ice would frequently back up against the aqueduct, and after the toll bridge was destroyed by ice flows in 1914, the center section of the aqueduct was removed and the two end sections bridged. This served as the bridge until the present bridge replaced it in 1964. The aqueduct was no longer necessary after the Barge Canal opened in 1917.

Horse-drawn carriage on DuBois Lane, Rexford, c. 1910. Stanley "Spud" Bartow took this photograph of his family out for a ride. Mrs. Bartow and daughters Bea and Irma are in the carriage.

Route 146, looking west toward the Nathan Garnsey (DeLong) House, Rexford, *c.* 1915. Clifton Park's main road was still a dirt road when this photograph was taken. Note the advertisement for Texaco Oil on the tree to the left.

"Home from church," Vischer Ferry Road, near Clifton Park Center, *c.* 1915. From left to right are: Mae and Lois Clark; their mother, Emeline Pattison Clark; and their brothers, Leicester, John, and George Clark. The family had just arrived home (see p. 27) from the Clifton Park Center Baptist Church (see p. 58).

"Robert in his courting buggy," Vischer Ferry Road, near Clifton Park Center, c. 1915. Robert Clark and Jerry the horse are shown in this family photograph. Note the large bouquet of flowers in the back of the buggy.

Railroad station and freight depot, Elnora, c. 1900. Elnora was an important freight depot on the D&H Railroad. Molasses arrived for Smith's Grain and Feed Store, and molding sand was loaded on the train for shipment to foundries. Mr. C.D. Hammond, supervisor of the D&H Railroad, named the community Elnora—after his wife—in 1882. It was previously known as Hubbs Corners. An overpass replaced the railroad crossing in the 1920s. A portion of this station still remains.

Belott Road, Elnora, 1914. A family is out enjoying a drive in their automobile. The license plate bears a 1914 date. Smith's Grain and Feed Store is in the distance on the left.

Near Jonesville, c. 1880. This tintype shows John B. Wood (left) and his son, Roland J. Wood. Roland (see p. 29) was the father of long-time Jonesville resident Vernon Wood.

Old Route 146 (Fire Road), west of Route 9, Clifton Park Village, *c.* 1900. This family photograph from the collection of George Dows of Clifton Park Village may show his father, Adam, out for a ride. The buildings are on the south side of Old Route 146. Note the lap robe for warmth.

Clifton Park Village, *c.* 1910. This could be George Dows of Clifton Park Village washing and polishing up his sporty buggy. Most residents of the town did not own automobiles until the late 1920s.

Clifton Park Village, c. 1910. From left to right are: (front seat) Thomas F. Bryar (at the wheel), Irene Andrews Rolen, and Adam L. Dows; (rear seat) Hattie Dows, George Dows, and Reba Horton Bryar (without hat). Written on the back of this postcard is: "Off for Ballston Fair-No start-Broken gas line-Finally made it." The car is a Winton, about 1908 to 1910.

Route 9, one mile south of Clifton Park Village, c. 1922. A major snowstorm delayed this bus on route to Montreal. Some local folks helped to shovel the bus out. Where were the snow plows?

Five

At Work

Farming, Vischer Ferry area, *c.* 1890. These farmers are threshing wheat, barley, or oats. The threshing machine is hooked up to a steam traction engine, which supplies the power to run the thresher. Until the 1960s, most of Clifton Park was an agrarian community.

Mr. Bell's sand team and men, Forts Ferry, c. 1890. On the back of this photograph Adam J. Van Vranken wrote, "Aunt G. [Gertrude Van Vranken Lansing], Miss Bell, Uncle John and men." The mining of molding sand was a major industry in Clifton Park during the late nineteenth and early twentieth centuries. The sand would be shipped out on canal boats or trains to foundries where it was used to produce cast iron.

Ice cutters on the Mohawk River, Mohawk View (south side of the river), *c.* 1900. In the days before electric refrigerators, ice was harvested in the winter, stored, and used throughout the year for home ice boxes. The New York Central Railroad used a lot of ice on their trains, and employed twenty to thirty local men (many from the Vischer Ferry area) to cut it and load it onto their freight cars. It was then delivered to ice houses.

Rioux ice house and District School No. 4, Clutes Dry Dock, *c.* 1900. The ice house is in back of the school. The large conveyor belt lifted the blocks of ice into the ice house for storage. Ice harvesting was done along the Mohawk River, and several ice houses existed in town.

Dry Dock, Erie Canal, Clutes Dry Dock, *c.* 1890. This view of the dry dock shows it drained of water so the cradles for holding the canal boats can be seen. A boat on the left is being repaired. The men are standing on the closed gates to the dry dock. The canal is just beyond, and Nicholas Clute's store is on the left. After boats entered the lock, the gates would be closed and the dry dock drained so that the boats could be repaired.

Work boat at the Coal Pocket, Erie Canal, Vischer Ferry, *c.* 1900. The work boat may have been the state boat that patrolled the canal between Crescent and Rexford to maintain the canal. Sometimes the boat would carry gravel to fill in the holes on the tow path. The Coal Pocket was located at the end of Ferry Drive, and was obviously a place where coal was stored, perhaps for steam-driven canal boats.

Peter's Mill, Crescent and Vischer Ferry Roads, c. 1890. Built by William Peters (see p. 14) in about 1814, this mill served a variety of purposes. It was used as a gristmill, sawmill, and a woolen mill. The mill was demolished in the 1920s, but the stone bridge still exists next to the new road.

Vischer's Mill, Ferry Drive, Vischer Ferry, c. 1900. The original mill at this location was established by Eldert Vischer by the time of the American Revolution. It is said that flour from this mill was used for the troops at the Battle of Saratoga in 1777. The mill pictured was probably the third Vischer mill located at this site, across the road from the Vischer homestead (see p. 14). It was taken down about 1950, but the foundation and mill stones are still visible.

Blacksmith shop, Vischer Ferry and Riverview Roads, Vischer Ferry, c. 1910. This postcard view is looking north up Vischer Ferry Road from the store. The blacksmith shop on the right may also have been a wagon shop, as you can see a large ramp to the rear of the building.

Elizabeth Van Vranken and John Wager, Riverview Road, Vischer Ferry, c. 1900. John Wager was a wood chopper for the people of Vischer Ferry. He was blind, and Elizabeth "Libby" Van Vranken would escort him around from place to place. If she was unable to do this, John could often find his own way by the various styles of fences, or by actually counting the number of pickets. It is remarkable that he had all of his fingers.

Idylwilde Orchards, Riverview Road east of Vischer Ferry, *c.* 1905. From left to right are: F. Ives, unknown, ? Shurly, unknown, Jerome Van Vranken (see p. 16), and George Van Vranken. Located on the farm of Abram Van Vranken, this peach orchard was operated by his sons.

Van Vranken, Undertaker, Riverview Road, Vischer Ferry, *c.* 1905. Garret and Brower Van Vranken were funeral directors for Vischer Ferry (see p. 44). This wagon served as a hearse, and provided one's last ride, to the cemetery.

Repairing the Erie Canal, Ferry Drive, Vischer Ferry, *c.* 1898. From left to right are: unknown, Mr. Odell, Mr. Potter, unknown, Mr. McKenzey (super on job), Mr. Wendell, and two unknown men. The water has been drained from the Erie Canal so that it can be repaired. The photograph is identified as "Contract 17 Erie Canal, T. H. Karr, Contractor." Note the approach and abutment to the canal bridge in the right background.

Lock 7 and dam, Barge Canal, Vischer Ferry, *c.* 1910. Construction of the Barge Canal began in 1907. Since it was to be in the Mohawk River, dams had to be built to make the river deeper. This postcard view, taken from the south side of the river, shows Lock 7 (in the foreground) and the dam, both under construction. The new Erie-Barge Canal opened in 1917, and the old Erie Canal was abandoned.

Stony Creek Reservoir, near Vischer Ferry, 1952. The Latham Water District purchased land in Clifton Park during the late 1940s to create a reservoir for the town of Colonie. This was a very controversial issue for Clifton Park and many of the local residents strongly opposed it. This view shows the construction of the dam that would hold back the waters of the Stony Creek (see p. 19).

William E. Rogers with a U.S. Mail Wagon, Rexford, c. 1900. Rural delivery of mail began in 1896. This early view shows the Rexford Flats mail wagon on its rounds.

Lock 20, Erie Canal, Riverview Landing, Rexford, *c.* 1885. Lock 20 was located about where Droms Road would intersect with the Mohawk River. This photograph shows one of the double chambers being lengthened so that two boats in tow could enter the lock at once. Hank Knowlton's hotel and store are in the background. This area was once known as Fundy's Basin. The lock is now underwater and can sometimes be seen when the river is low.

Lock 21, Erie Canal, Rexford, *c.* 1885. One of the chambers of this double lock is being lengthened to accommodate two boats in tow. This was done to most all of the Erie Canal locks around 1885. Rexford is in the distance.

Repairing the aqueduct, Erie Canal, Rexford, *c*. 1894. From left to right are: (front row) James Collins (division superintendent) and Pat Mulligan (foreman); (middle row) George Cohn, unknown, Mr. Shannesey, Richard Clute, and other unidentified men; (back row) John Ice, Henry Crane (state driver), unknown, James Scanlon, James Connally, and other unidentified men. These workmen posed on a cold winter day to record their work on the aqueduct. The aqueduct had to be repaired during the winter months when it was not in use.

C.H. Schmidt Blacksmith Shop, Main Street, Rexford, *c*. 1900. The man in the middle wearing a leather apron is probably C.H. Schmidt, the blacksmith. There were several blacksmith shops in Rexford. The building on the right was Redman Hall, used as the Elks Club (see p. 39). The photographer was John Rogers (see p. 23).

Repairing Route 146, Rexford, c. 1915. A road crew fixes the road near the Nathan Garnsey (DeLong) House on Route 146. Note the jackets flung over the fence.

Painting the Nathan Garnsey (DeLong) House, Route 146, Rexford, c. 1895. These painters are painting a red brick house white, the color it remains today (see p. 24).

John P. Clark on a hay rake, Clark Farm, Vischer Ferry Road, near Clifton Park Center, 1911 (see p. 27). Haying was a major job in Clifton Park's agriculture-based economy.

The last load of hay, Clark Farm, Vischer Ferry Road, near Clifton Park Center, 1911 (see p. 27). Members of the Clark family loaded on the wagon include, from left to right: Robert, George, Mae, Lois, mother Emeline Pattison Clark, and Leicester. Standing in front of the wagon is father John P. Clark.

Feeding chickens, Carlson Farm, Moe Road near Englemore Road, 1913. Edna, Ted, and Agnes Carlson are feeding the chickens, a common chore for children. Their father purchased the old Abraham Moe farm in 1906.

Firemen in front of the Horstman Barn, MacElroy Road, Jonesville, c. 1922. From left to right, in front of Jonesville's first fire truck (a 1922 American LaFrance), are: (standing) unknown, unknown, Roland Hubbs, Dan Mead, Al Knorowski, Chief Kenny Noyes, unknown, unknown, Douglas MacElroy, and unknown. The Jonesville Fire Department was formed in 1919.

Dr. John R. MacElroy in his office, Main Street, Jonesville, *c.* 1950. Dr. MacElroy, a well-known country doctor, began his career in Jonesville in 1894 and practiced medicine there for over sixty years. He was known to generations of Jonesville patients, hundreds of whom he brought into this world. In 1950, he was elected as the State Medical Association's first "Outstanding General Practitioner of the Year."

Adam Dows' Sawmill, Clifton Park Village, *c.* 1905. From left to right are: Adam Dows, possibly Thomas F. Bryar, and George Dows (Adam's son, see p. 86).

Blacksmith and Carriage Shop, Old Route 146 (Fire Road), Clifton Park Village, *c*. 1890. This building stood on the site of the present Clifton Park Fire House. The sporty vehicles out front are probably for sale.

Six

At Play

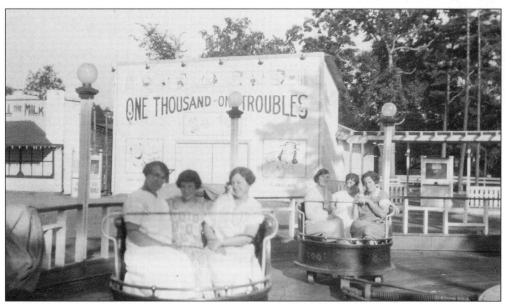

Rexford Amusement Park, Rexford, September 1926. These ladies riding the whip are enjoying the concessionaires clambake. Looking east over the whip, from left to right we can see: Spill the Milk; the Hall of Mirrors; and the aerial swing in its new location in the corner of the park, on the river bluff. The amusement park opened in 1906 as Luna Park; after Fred Dolle acquired it in 1911, the name was changed to Dolle's Park. In 1916 the park came under new management as Rexford Park. It closed after the 1933 season. The park was located on the river, just west of the village of Rexford.

Van Vranken family picnic on the Mohawk River, west of Forts Ferry, July 4, 1895. The matriarch, Dorcas Cragier (Mrs. John W.) Van Vranken, is seated in the center of this group, sixth from the left, behind the watermelon. She is surrounded by her children, grandchildren, and great-grandchildren. At her left may be her son, William Halloway Van Vranken, and his wife, Susan Fort Van Vranken.

Yacht *Elscey*, Mohawk River, west of Forts Ferry, July 4, 1895. This photograph was taken the same day as the one at the top of the page. William Halloway and Susan Fort Van Vranken ran a boarding house up on Riverview Road (see p. 16), and used the riverfront for picnicking, swimming, and boating. The yacht *Elscey* was named for their daughter, Carrie Elscey, born in 1882.

Bath 3 Club, Mohawk River, west of Forts Ferry, *c.* 1900. William Halloway and Susan Fort Van Vranken allowed a group of boys from Cohoes to use their cabin on the river one summer. In return, the boys made a photo album of local views, some of which are used in this book.

Family gathering, Riverview Road, Vischer Ferry, *c.* 1900. These folks are sitting in the front yard of the house across from the Amity Church. This house was later used as a funeral parlor by Brower and Elsie Van Vranken. The parents appear to be seated on either end.

Picnickers on the bridge over the sluice-way to the Vischer Mill, Vischer Ferry, July 4, 1891. The man in the center with the guitar may be Ben Howd, who lived in the Greek Revival home near the intersection of Crescent and Vischer Ferry Roads, now 34 Vischer Ferry Road.

Picnickers on the mill pond dam, Vischer Ferry, July 4, 1891. Some of the same people in the previous photograph appear in this one, including the man with the guitar. Vischer Ferry was a popular resort at this time. This is a good view of the mill pond, which continued up behind the store. The pond was drained about 1905.

Dinner at the Gillette's, Grooms Corners, c. 1905. Belle and George Gillette are at left, and their daughter Hazel is on the right. The other lady is unknown. It appears to be a turkey on the table. Perhaps they are celebrating Thanksgiving or Christmas (see p. 20).

Installation of officers, Juvenile Grange, Grange Hall, Grooms Corners, 1948. From left to right are: (front row) Pauline Merrill, Genevieve Merrill, and Marilyn Turner; (back row) Gerald Turner, Don Carlson, Mrs. Perkins, Delbert (Jack) Merrill, and Virginia Turner. The Grange was an important organization in an agrarian community like Clifton Park (see p. 37).

Lock 22, Erie Canal, Rexford, *c.* 1905. This postcard view is titled, "Down in the Locks." A corner of the Travis Store (see p. 53) can be seen on the right, and the McKain House (see p. 23) is on the cliff in the background. It was evidently a popular pastime to watch the boats go through the locks. Judging by the number of people on the boat, this may have been a special excursion, or perhaps they were merely catching a free ride through the lock.

Lock 22, Erie Canal, Rexford, *c.* 1910. All eyes seem to be on the speed boat, although the *Eureka* looks like a nifty pleasure boat as well. It seems like quite a crowd gathered at the lock.

Bea and Irma Bartow, Rexford, July 4, *c.* 1910 (see p. 81). Independence Day was an important event in Clifton Park and was celebrated with parades, family picnics, and hoopla. Today, the Fourth of July is still celebrated in grand style in Clifton Park.

Tracy's Fire Works Stand, Rexford, *c.* 1930. Homer Tracy, dressed in white, is shown here with his wife and children. This stand was located on the northeast side of the Rexford bridge. Fireworks were evidently legal at this time.

Gertrude Boyce on the porch of her father's store, Rexford, c. 1910. Playing with dolls has always been a favorite pastime of little girls. Gertrude's father ran the store formerly owned by George Eaton (see p. 51). Did another relative run the store in Clifton Park Village (see p. 66)?

A rented "Hathaway," Riverview Road, west of Route 146, Rexford, c. 1900. This rented vehicle takes a group of young people on an outing in Rexford. The house in the background still stands on Riverview Road near the Alplaus line.

Trolley stop, Rexford Amusement Park, Rexford, *c.* 1920. The electric trolley stop can be seen in the left foreground. Trolley lines all over the United States brought city folk to amusement parks (see pp. 2, 80, and 103). The main entrance is between the two large posts. Note the roller coaster on the left and the merry-go-round on the right. The aerial swing ride can be seen behind the merry-go-round to the right.

Amusement park ride, Luna Park, Rexford, *c.* 1906. The man on the right appears to be operating this ride by using a rope to spin it. Note the other ropes hanging from the ride which he probably grabs in succession. A Wurlitzer barrel organ provides loud music.

Silhouettist, Luna Park, Rexford, *c.* 1906. The man at right is cutting a silhouette of the woman posed on the left. Several admiring onlookers watch from behind.

Shoot-the-Chute, Luna Park, Rexford, *c.* 1906. This ride was an earlier interpretation of the log flume ride where you ride a car down the steep slope into the pool, and everyone gets wet. Note the trolley tracks and station on the left. They cut through the park.

Ice Cream Parlor, Rexford Park, Rexford, c. 1920. It looks like the workers are ready to wait on us. Perhaps this photograph was taken before the start, or at the end, of a busy day.

Train ride, Rexford Park, Rexford, September 1926. The concessionaires are enjoying their clambake (see p. 103). The train ran in front of the Grand View Hotel and then back east through a swampy area. The building is the picnic area. A small aerial swing is at the rear, and a tilt-a-whirl can be seen in the distance.

Refreshment stand, Rexford Park, Rexford, *c.* 1920. This refreshment stand offered lemonade for 10¢ a glass. On the right is the Grand View Hotel, built in 1901 by Jacob Rupert, the New York City brewery king. This began the development of the amusement park.

Grandview Hotel fire, Rexford (formerly Luna) Park, Rexford, *c.* 1925. Note the Luna Park sign on the lamp pole in the foreground.

William Graves and his friends at a clambake with in the woods near Rexford, *c.* 1900. William Graves is the fifth from the front (partially hidden, with a straw hat, mustache, and shirtsleeves). He was married to Fannie Rexford, daughter of Cyrus and Hannah Rexford (see p. 22). One wonders what special event prompted this gentleman's clambake.

DeLong tea party, Nathan Garnsey (DeLong) House, Route 146, Rexford, *c.* 1900 (see pp. 24 and 116). Henry C. DeLong is seated at right, and his wife, Millie Smalley DeLong, is seated second from right. Third from right is their son, Harry Nathan DeLong. Harry's sister, Edna DeLong Dyer, is serving tea, and her son Royal is the boy at left. Harry Nathan DeLong is LeGrand DeLong's father.

Centennial Anniversary (1791–1891), Nathan Garnsey (DeLong) House, Route 146, Rexford, September 1891. Standing to the right of the large tree beneath the welcome sign is Millie Smalley DeLong, a granddaughter of John Smalley and Hannah Barnes (niece of Nathan Garnsey Jr.), with her husband, Henry C. DeLong, owners of the house. To the right of Mr. DeLong is an unknown man, then LeGrand Rexford, and Cyrus W. Rexford. Emmor J. Caldwell is seated in the second row, sixth from left, and in front of him to the left is Garnsey Caldwell, seated in the first row, fourth from left. The others are friends and relatives, many of them descendants of Nathan Garnsey who built the house in 1791 (see p. 24). Route 146 appears as a one-lane road.

Bicentennial Anniversary, (1791–1991), Nathan Garnsey (DeLong) House, Route 146, Rexford, September 7, 1991. George and Marilyn DeLong Hubbard, owners of the house, are standing in the doorway. In front of them are Willard and Julienne DeLong Sproat and their daughters, Diane and Deborah. Marilyn and Julienne, daughters of LeGrand and Rochelle DeLong, are great granddaughters of Henry and Millie Smally DeLong, who had the 100th anniversary party in 1891 (see preceding page). A granddaughter, Jeannette DeLong Magnussen, sister of LeGrand DeLong, is seated in the second row, fourth from the right. The lady wearing a necklace, seated at center in front of Julienne and Diane Sproat, is Ann Caldwell; left of her is Nathan D. Caldwell, and then her husband Emmor J. Caldwell. Standing left of Emmor is David Garnsey Caldwell holding his daughter Kari. Kari's brother Caleb is just behind her. The Caldwells are descendants of Nathan Garnsey, the builder of the house in 1791. The others are friends and relatives.

LeGrand DeLong, Nathan Garnsey (DeLong) House, Route 146, Rexford, 1930. Hunting is still a popular pastime with town residents. This brand new, shiny Model-A Ford was unfortunately scratched by the antlers of the deer. LeGrand recounted this story to his daughters. Alas, the price to pay for bagging a deer.

Refreshment stand, Forest Park, Ballston Lake, c. 1910. Forest Park opened in 1904 at the south end of the lake. Like the amusement park in Rexford, it was a result of a trolley line which brought people from the cities on evenings and weekends to enjoy new-found leisure time. There was a merry-go-round and a dance pavilion. Canoes could be rented, and there was swimming. Many folks from Clifton Park spent time here before the park closed in the 1930s.

Ballston Lake from Forest Park, *c.* 1910. Although the dock from which this postcard view was taken is in the town of Ballston, the opposite shore is in the town of Clifton Park. In fact, with a magnifying glass you can see the rooftop of the "Castle" (see p. 26) with a flag flying over it. The *Comanche* was a steam-driven tour boat that plied the lake from Forest Park.

GE "Test" men engineers at Camp "Summer Rest," Ballston Lake, *c.* 1920. B.G. Hatch owned this camp on the east side of Ballston Lake, along East Side Drive. Every summer he would invite his GE colleagues to spend a week or two at his camp. Today, many of these camps have become year-round homes.

Eating watermelon, Clark Farm, Vischer Ferry Road, near Clifton Park Center, c. 1910. Standing in back from the left are John P. Clark and his wife, Emeline Pattison Clark. The boy in the center may be their son Leicester (see pp. 27 and 82).

Playing croquet, Clark Farm, Vischer Ferry Road, near Clifton Park Center, c. 1910. Scott and Blanche Pattison were probably the nephew and niece of Emeline Pattison Clark. Croquet was a very popular game at the turn of the century.

Family reunion at the home of Roland J. Wood (see p. 29), Main Street, Jonesville, c. 1925. Seated on the ground at left is Roland J. Wood (see p. 84). His granddaughter, Hulda Bloodgood, is seated next to him. Vernon Woods, a son of Roland and a long-time Jonesville resident, may be in the back row wearing a striped shirt and tie. Family reunions were popular summertime events, often held annually.

National Beagle Club, Jonesville Hotel, Main Street and MacElroy Road, Jonesville, October 11, 1912. Dr. John MacElroy (see p. 101) started a local chapter of the National Beagle Club. Members would come by train to the Elnora station, and stay overnight at the Jonesville Hotel. Field trials were held to test the ability of the dogs to improve the strains of Beagles. The rabbit field trials were held in the Jonesville Cemetery and bush country southwest of town.

Methodist church clambake, Jonesville, September 4, 1922. The man at man in front at the bake table (with straw hat) is Mr. Weatherill. Partially visible to the right of him is Roland Hubbs. The boy to the left of Mr. Weatherill is Donald MacElroy, whose father, Dr. John MacElroy, and mother, Claire MacElroy), are seated at the end of the table just behind him. Roy Noyes is the next man standing (wearing coat, tie, and hat) to the right of Mr. Weatherill. The man on the right of the bake table wearing suspenders is John Henry Riddle, and just behind him on the right is Frank Warner. Behind Riddle on the left is Cornell Burke. Moving to the center of the photograph, standing on the right side of the center table, from the right are

Ted Carlson with baseball bat, Moe Road near Englemore Road, c. 1920. Baseball was as popular then as it is today. The barn in back still stands. It was originally one of Thomas Edison's laboratories in Schenectady, and was moved to the Carlson farm for use as a barn.

Grace Weatherill (wife of Mr. Weatherill), Maude Hubbs, and Mr. Filkins. On the other side of the table leaning against a tree is Harry Nathan DeLong. Carrie Birch DeLong is standing at the rear of the table on the left, by the front corner of the church, and under the ice cream sign at the very left of the photograph is Sarah Smith. Practically every resident of Jonesville is in this photograph. The Methodist church clambakes at Jonesville were famous. They were an annual Labor Day tradition from 1896 to 1960. If it rained, the church sheds behind the church were used. After they were torn down, it was necessary to use Odd Fellows Hall or the firehouse on a rainy day.

George Dows, dressed up and fishing, Route 9, Clifton Park Village, *c.* 1900. George is pictured in a top hat, fishing from a pail in his home in Clifton Park. He lived all his life in Clifton Park Village, and preserved many old photographs and artifacts relating to the area. Some of these photographs appear in this book (see pp. 85, 86, and 101).

Fourth of July Parade, Old Route 146 and Route 9, Clifton Park Village, c. 1890. Independence Day has always been a major holiday in Clifton Park, celebrated with parades, family picnics (see pp. 104 and 106), and hoopla. The traditional parade route seems to have been along Old Route 146 (Fire Road), turning south on Route 9 before the Clifton Park Hotel. The lead wagon exibits a sign announcing the Clifton Park Sewing Circle. The Clifton Park Hotel displays a welcome banner.

Fourth of July Parade, Old Route 146 and Route 9, Clifton Park Village, 1917. The parade has just turned the corner from Old Route 146 (Fire Road) and is headed south on Route 9. The float in the foreground is carrying veterans of the Civil and Spanish-American Wars. A sign on the float reads: "Rally Round the Flag Boys." The building on the left is the store and post office (see p. 67), the hotel sheds are in the center, and on the right is a corner of the Clifton Park Hotel.

Fourth of July Parade, Old Route 146 and Route 9, Clifton Park Village, 1918. The car is decorated with flags and red, white, and blue streamers. The ladies in the car are wearing fancy red, white, and blue bonnets. Even the Clifton Park Hotel is decked out in bunting.

Fourth of July Parade, Old Route 146 and Route 9, Clifton Park Village, c. 1920. This appears to be a local chapter of the Klu Klux Klan complete with hoods. The Klan was especially active in upstate New York during the 1920s.

Dedication of the war monument, Old Route 146 and Route 9, looking south, c. Memorial Day or July 4, 1919. The Clifton Park war monument, dedicated to those who served in World War I, stood in the center of Old Route 146, in front of the Clifton Park Hotel. It was probably removed when Route 9 was widened. The building on the left is now Snyder's Restaurant. The view is looking down Route 9. A parlor organ is set up on a temporary stage to provide music for the occasion.

Merwin Wood (left) and George T. Dows, Clifton Park Village, c. 1908. Merwin is holding a pet chicken and George is pulling a large wonderfully decorated wagon, demonstrating what children did in the days before television and computer games.

Boy Scout Troop 28 at ground-breaking ceremonies for the Shenendehowa Central School, August 1952. From left to right are: Jack Merrill, Ted Carlson (assistant scoutmaster), Tommy Powers, Lloyd Tourtelot, Dick Jerome, Alan Palmer, Charlie Wickes, possibly Walt Whinnery, Don Carlson, unknown, Gordon Peck, Bill Beck, George (Buddy) Gage, Gerald Turner, unknown little boy, Peter Fasake, Phil Dean, unknown, unknown, Bruce Jerome, Al Myers, and Vic Knorowski. Shenendehowa was the Indian name for the Clifton Park land patent of 1708. The first building for 1,470 pupils cost $2,535,000, and was first occupied in September 1953. Boy Scouts and Girl Scouts have always been popular with Clifton Park youth. Troop 28 was sponsored by the Clifton Park Baptist Church.

Shenendehowa Community Chorus, Gowana School, c. 1954. Peg Morse (on the right) was the director. Second from the right is Anne Carlson. Judging from the Christmas tree, it must have been a holiday concert. Music has always been a popular leisure-time activity, with local groups ranging from church choirs to community bands.

Acknowledgments

Many of the images in this volume come from the town's valuable collection, made possible largely by former Clifton Park Town Historian Howard I. Becker (1894–1978). Others have provided additional photographs from family collections. I am grateful to the following for allowing me to use and copy valuable family photographs: Frank Berlin, Don Berthiaume, George Dows Collection, Elmer Droms, Charles and Marilyn Eells (Gillette family), George and Marilyn Hubbard (Garnsey Family), Judith Carlson Kleinburg (Carlson family), Donald MacElroy, Hulda Olsen (Wood and Vischer families), John and Grace Palm, Dr. Elizabeth Peck, Margery Shaw (Clark family), Edgar and Mary Shopmyer, Andrea Weening (Schauber family), and Virginia Whetton. The Saratoga County Historical Society provided the photograph of the Elnora freight station.

Craig Williams, my colleague at the New York State Museum, provided copy prints of some extraordinary canal photographs from the Museum collection. Ross Shepherd, Jonesville Fire Department, assisted in identifying people in the photograph of the Jonesville clambake, 1922, and gave me leads to locate other material. John Papp of Schenectady allowed me to use a photograph of a mule-pulled canal boat at Vischer Ferry, and Dan Cole, also of Schenectady, provided some computer-enhanced photographs of Rexford.

Assistance in identifying photographs was rendered by Ted Carlson, Don Carlson, Judith Carlson Kleinburg, Bruce Jerome, Catherine Molnar, Ken and Lydia Noyes, Isabel Prescott, Jean Ward, and Ron and Gail Winters.

A very special thank you is due to two special friends and collaborators who share my love of local history. Doris Cole has been preserving the history of Rexford for many years. She generously provided me with some wonderful photographs of the Rexford area, and shared her wealth of knowledge of that area. I am truly grateful for all her help and support on this book.

The other special thank you goes to William Van Vranken of New Jersey, a descendant of the Fort and Van Vranken families, Clifton Park's first families. I have come to look forward to Bill's visits on his way through town, and listening to his stories of life at Fort's Ferry and Vischer Ferry when he was a boy. Fortunately, Bill has preserved and identified all his family photographs, many documenting late-nineteenth-century life at Fort's Ferry and Vischer Ferry. I am truly grateful to him for making this valuable collection available for this book.

Finally, I must acknowledge the assistance and patience of my family. My wife, Martha, son Andy, and daughter Amy have been my best critics. They particularly helped in selecting some 225 photographs from a total of 400. They gave me an objective response as to which photographs were better or more interesting than others, a difficult task, indeed.